My name is...
Picasso

© Copyright 2006 of English translation by Barron's Educational Series, Inc. for the United States, its territories and possessions, and Canada.

Original title of the book in Spanish: *Me llamo...Picasso*
© 2004 Parramón Ediciones, S.A.,—World Rights
Published by Parramón Ediciones, S.A., Barcelona, Spain

Name of the author of the text: Eva Bargalló
Name of the illustrator: Violeta Monreal

Translated from the Spanish by Eric A. Bye, M.A.

Project and Production: Parramón Publishing
Editorial Director: Lluís Borràs
Editorial Assistant: Cristina Vilella
Text: Eva Bargalló
Illustrations: Violeta Monreal
Graphic Design and Layout: Zink Communications, Inc.
Production Director: Rafael Marfil
Production: Manel Sánchez

All inquiries should be addressed to:
Barron's Educational Series, Inc.
250 Wireless Boulevard
Hauppauge, New York 11788
www.barronseduc.com

ISBN-13: 978-0-7641-3393-0
ISBN-10: 0-7641-3393-4

Library of Congress Catalog Card No.: 2005929510

Printed in Spain

9 8 7 6 5 4 3 2 1

Hello...

Even though I am famous because of my paintings, I must say that I owe part of my celebrity to the fact that I have known many interesting people and I lived many years during a time—a major part of the twentieth century—that was one of the most exciting ones from a cultural standpoint. It was like finishing an old book and starting a different one filled with new ideas and a look toward the future. The new representatives of culture learned from those who went before, but we also challenged their knowledge, and we sought a new language more appropriate for modern times. Unfortunately, this was also a period of bloody wars, injured societies, and conflicts between peoples.

I experienced all of this firsthand, and I was even one of the major players. My restless and independent character, combined with my inborn gifts for artistic creation, pushed me to search for new languages of expression, without compromising with anyone, and that made me the greatest artist of the twentieth century. At least that's what the experts say!

Anyway, I can't complain. I lived an intense life in which painting, women, and bulls were my main passions, and on occasion, my downfall, and my memory will always linger in the minds of the people who pause in front of a work with my signature on it.

Surrounded by Women in My Childhood

I was born in the nineteenth century, specifically on October 25, 1881, in Málaga, Spain. This Andalusian city is bathed by the Mediterranean Sea, which wraps the daily life of the inhabitants in happiness and color. Because of its port, this once was a prosperous and dynamic city. During the years of my childhood, however, it was suffering from a poor economy that could not be overcome until many decades later, but that's another story. I merely want to say that at the end of the nineteenth century it was a culturally backward city.

It is said that I was a very lively child, and that my talent for drawing blossomed at a very early age. My father, José Ruiz Blasco, was a drawing teacher at the San Telmo School of Fine Arts, so I inherited his love of art. He was already a mature man of forty-three when I was born; his character was quiet, and sometimes a little gloomy. In contrast, my mother, Maria Picasso López, seventeen years younger than my father, was cheerful and optimistic.

My first years in this world passed by happily despite the economic difficulties that we experienced. A teacher's salary at that time was quite little. However, the affectionate care that the countless female members of my family gave me made me a happy, sparkling boy whose favorite pastimes were playing and drawing. You know, every child is an artist. The problem is how to remain an artist once he or she grows up. In addition, I soon had two new playmates: my sisters Lola and Concepcion.

From my father I inherited a taste not only for drawing, but also for bulls and doves. Now do you see why I pictured them so frequently in my works? In fact, one of my first paintings, *The Picador*, depicts a scene inspired by a bullfight.

I don't recall precisely when I painted it, but I think it was around 1890, when I was eight or nine years old. And concerning the doves, what better tribute than to name my daughter after them, and to do drawings of them that have traveled around the world several times and have been used as symbols of peace? Among all my works in which doves appear, I remember with particular fondness *Girl with Dove*, which I painted at the beginning of the twentieth century in Paris, which at that time was the worldwide center of art.

The Sky Becomes Tinged with Gray

In 1891 my father got a position as professor in the Da Guarda School of Fine Arts in a place named La Coruña. This change required us to move to Galicia, so we had to leave the Mediterranean and its brightness. I also left behind me forever the sweetness and innocence of childhood. It is said that here I fell in love for the first time; that may be, but it was so long ago.

Given my enthusiasm and my talent for painting, my father decided that I should begin to study art in an official school, so they enrolled me in the school where he was teaching; he thus came to be one of my many teachers as well as my adviser.

During those adolescent years spent under the overcast sky of La Coruña, my exceptional artistic skills were realized. At least that's what my father thought—he decided to give me his brushes and to give up forever the pleasure of painting. *The Sick Woman* and *Country Scene* date from that period, 1894–1895; those works already show my desire to create different languages for expression.

Our stay in Galicia wasn't as peaceful as we had hoped. My father's salary wasn't enough to live comfortably on (in fact, I experienced economic difficulties up to the age of twenty-five), and we longed for the land where we had grown up. However, the worst was yet to come, for at the end of 1894 my little sister Concepcion caught diphtheria, and she died on January 10, 1895 The death of such a young and beloved person was a traumatic experience that filled our home and our hearts with sadness. Later the same year, I did a portrait of the doctor who took care of her, Dr. Perez Costales, a family friend. I think I succeeded in capturing his solemn character, and that the lines and dark colors express the sadness that possessed me at the time.

A few months later, in the summer of the same year, we packed our bags and headed for Málaga so we could spend all our vacation there, and then we moved to our new destination: Barcelona. En route to Andalucia we passed through Madrid, and even though we didn't stop to spend the night there, we did visit the Prado Museum. For the first time my eyes could delight in the works of the old masters: El Greco, Velazquez, Goya... I was so impressed that several years later I returned to study these geniuses of painting in greater depth. But let's not get ahead of ourselves—we need to go one step at a time.

Discovering Modernity: Barcelona

At the end of September 1895, we headed for Barcelona and set up home in the old part of town, specifically on a street near the port and the train station. Condal City was in the middle of being transformed. Modernism began in places such as Paris, Vienna, and London, which allowed artists and architects to create new shapes of movement with the construction of the Urban Expansion Area. The rising middle class turned the city into the most modern one in Spain, not just from a technological viewpoint, but from an intellectual one as well. The proof of that was the Universal Exposition of 1888, which changed the fortress at Barcelona into a recreation area with beautiful gardens and amazing pavilions.

Thanks to help by some of the great families of the time, artists like Gaudi left us such imposing buildings as La Pedrera and the Holy Family, and painters such as Rusinol, Casas, and Nonell were able to incorporate the new style of the French Impressionists into their paintings.

For a boy like me—who at that time didn't know anything more than the academic studies of the fine arts schools of local cities—the possibility of living in such an environment meant opening the door to a new universe of art and culture, filled with surprises, and whose most distant and unknown corners took me a whole lifetime to explore.

But we didn't talk only of art and culture. At the end of the nineteenth century, new, revolutionary political ideas were sprouting up in Europe and were also simmering in the kitchens of Barcelona—such as anarchism and communism. And all this was going on in the light of two new discoveries: electricity, which turned night into day and darkness into light, and the moving picture, which became a strong influence on my conception of the language of art.

Years of Study

So 3 Reina Cristina Street was my first address in Barcelona. Once we had moved in, I resumed my art studies at the school where my father was teaching, the Barcelona School of Fine Arts, popularly referred to as La Llotja. Great artists passed through its classrooms, including Joan Miró, whom I admired and who succeeded in creating an expressive language that demonstrated the freedom of childhood and carried the fantastic imagery of the art of Surrealism.

At the Llotja, in addition to learning about painting, I came to understand the value of friendship. Manuel Pallarès, who was five years older than I was, became my inseparable friend in studies and travel. Our friendship lasted for seventy-eight years, until my death in 1973.

From him I came to know the various sides of a sparkling Barcelona: the happy life of the Paralelo, the easygoing environment of the taverns... And I shared my first studio and my stays in Horta de Ebro, in Tarragona, with him.

In April of 1896, before leaving for Málaga on summer vacation, I took part in the Barcelona Fine Arts and Art Industries Exposition with a painting that featured my sister Lola at her first communion. If you want to see it, it's displayed in the museum in Barcelona that bears my name.

After returning from Málaga, we decided to move to Mercè Street, very close to where we were, and I opened my first workshop at 4 Plata Street. This inauguration was a milestone in my life—it began my independence from my family, and my freedom as a person and an artist. And before my big move to Paris, there were other workshops, all in the old part of the city, the area where I developed from adolescence to young adulthood.

A Treasure Enclosed in Four Walls

The First Communion was not the only painting I exhibited in a contest. In June of 1897, I tried my luck once again with the oil painting *Science and Charity*, which I exhibited in the General Exhibition of Fine Arts in Madrid. I got an honorable mention! This recognition of my work motivated me to enroll in the San Fernando School of Fine Arts in Madrid, which had a long academic tradition. However, I didn't like what they were teaching there. I knew I could break out of the mold of academic painting that was being taught in the official centers. I wanted to show that art doesn't just have one language and that too many rules limit an artist's creativity. Everything you can imagine is real. Instead of following the strict academic schedule, I devoted as much time as possible to painting on my own and getting to know the paintings that hung on the walls of the Prado Museum. This ancient palace was my favorite refuge during my brief stay in Madrid, since the cultural environment in that city at the end of the nineteenth century was not the same as that of Barcelona. It took several decades and lots of history for Madrid to finally reach the cultural importance it deserved.

I want to thank the staff of the Prado Museum for the opportunity, many years later, to exhibit my works beside others done by the painters I admired so much, such as Velázquez, Miró, and Gris, in an exhibit of Spanish portraiture from the fifteenth to the twentieth century. And at the risk of appearing vain, I also want to congratulate its organizers for having chosen, among others, the portrait I did of Gertrude Stein in 1906. People tell the story that when Gertrude Stein saw the finished work, she expressed her doubts that she looked like it, and I answered, "Don't worry, you will."

But let's get back to the thread of the story. In June of 1898, while still in Madrid, I became ill with scarlet fever. Destiny brought me back to my beloved Barcelona, although only for a brief time, for in 1904, I would settle permanently in Paris.

Horta de Ebro

The scarlet fever left me so weak that my friend Pallarès was able to convince me to spend my time convalescing in his native town: Horta de Ebro. I couldn't imagine how important the long stay in this beautiful place located at the foot of the Ports de Besseit, in the province of Tarragona, would be for me and my artistic career. The impact that the rough landscape, the colors, the special architecture of the houses, and the rural surroundings produced on me kept me in that place for eight months.

I took advantage of the peace and the unhurried pace of time in Horta to do several drawings and paintings.

Long afterward, the critics who have specialized in studying my work agreed that in this place I developed for the first time the language that later would become known as Cubism. It is also certain that at some point I said that everything I know I learned in the town of Horta. It's possible to say that, because after a few years I went back there, and I did several paintings with which I really am very satisfied, such as *The Factory* and *The Irrigation Pond at Horta*. Art critics who like to classify things have defined them as belonging to Geometric Cubism.

I was also pleasantly surprised because I have learned that the kind people of Horta have created a center that brings together everything about the creation of my work associated with that place.

Els Quatre Gats

I returned to Barcelona in February of 1899, entirely recovered and eager to take part in the cultural life of the city and to strike up friendships and relationships with the artists and intellectuals of the time.

But where could I go to contact the intellectuals of Barcelona? There was only one place that had all the conditions to satisfy my desire for knowledge, growth, and new ideas: Els Quatre Gats (The Four Cats). This charming establishment, which was a tavern, brewery, and countless other things, opened its doors in June of 1897. Its owner, Pere Romeu, deserves credit for having attracted the upper crust of Barcelona's culture. His customers included a long list of other people from all artistic and literary disciplines. Among them are two names I wish to emphasize: the painter Carles Casagemas, with whom I would share a workshop in Riera de Sant Joan and the experience of my first trip to Paris, and the poet Jaume Sabartès, who eventually would become my personal secretary.

The walls of Els Quatre Gats were covered with paintings and drawings of the customers who frequented the tavern. A mural painted by Ramon Casas was remarkable for its size, its style, and its visual impact; it showed Pere Romeu and the painter mounted on a tandem bicycle.

Thanks to the kindness of Pere Romeu, in February of 1900 I organized my first solo exposition in the rooms of this intimate space. I chose some portraits I had done of my friends and companions from our gatherings. If you are interested in knowing the people who attended these evening sessions and with whom I shared experiences and conversations, you can take a trip into the past by looking at the portraits I painted during this period.

Paris, the Center of Art

When I was almost nineteen, I once again felt the need for a change of scenery. This time the chosen place was Paris: the city of light, art, cabarets, and the Universal Exposition of 1900. In May of that year an excuse to travel to the French capital was presented to me on a platter: my painting *Last Moments* was to be exhibited in the Spanish section of the Exposition. So in the fall my friend Casagemas and I took a train to Paris. What a surprise when we got off the train and saw the spectacular and modern Orsay train station, a metal structure that housed sixteen tracks, elevators, freight elevators, and other fantastic contrivances! Of course you may already know that some time ago the trains left the tracks of this beautiful station forever, and that this tremendous space now houses one of the most popular museums in Paris.

The three short months that my first stay in Paris lasted were enough to leave me dazzled with the cultural environment that filled its streets. Museums, expositions, gatherings, relationships with artists... and especially, the pleasure of contemplating the works of the great French painters.

My first painting done on French soil, *Le Moulin de la Galette* (not to be confused with a painting with the same name by the Impressionist painter Renoir) perfectly reflects the influence that this first direct contact with Impressionism and the Parisian nighttime environment had on me.

I had another pleasant experience during this trip: I got
to know the Catalan Pere Mañach, who became interested
in my paintings and offered me his services as an agent. Do
you know what an agent does? That's the person who acts as an
intermediary between artists and the purchasers of their works.
In truth, my paintings were quickly to become so highly sought
after in the art marketplace that I would become a rich man.
However, before that happened, I experienced some times of
great instability and poverty.

In December of 1900 I returned to Barcelona. Casagemas, sad
and depressed by the unrequited love he felt for a model he
had met in Paris, spent Christmas with me. I had no way of
knowing how fatally his heart was broken. Unfortunately, it
didn't take me long to find out: two months later, on February
17, 1901, while I was in Madrid, my dear friend took his life,
and I couldn't do anything to help him.

The Sadness of the Color Blue

The year 1901 was a crucial time in my life and work. To begin with, I decided to sign my paintings with my mother's last name. Although this may appear to be an insignificant detail at this point, it was an important step; the proof is that today I am known all around the world by the name Picasso.

I also decided to return to Paris. I did so in June, for at the end of that month I was having my first show in the French capital at the Vollard Gallery. But neither the success nor the fame I achieved rescued me from the depths into which I had fallen. Even though I fit perfectly into the artistic environment of the city and turned into a steady customer of the cafés and the dance salons, the death of Casagemas and a lack of money kept me from seeing the good side of life. Instead, it seemed that my world had suddenly become filled with beggars, sick people, old people... Sadness and solitude had taken over my heart, and despite my frequent trips to Barcelona, I couldn't pull myself from that long tunnel I had gotten myself into.

At that time, my only safety valve was painting. The color blue invaded my paintings. I focused on drawing men and women whose faces and bodies communicated the unrest and sadness that I felt at the time. Many years later, it was said that the work I did during this time, which is referred to as the Blue Period, was the most personal and introspective of my entire production, and that the influence of El Greco is clearly visible in it. Do you know who El Greco was? He was a great painter of the sixteenth century. I have already mentioned how impressed I was with his works in the Prado Museum in Madrid.

If I had to choose the two paintings that express most precisely my state of mind at that time, I think I would choose a self-portrait I did in 1901 and the oil painting *Life*, which I painted in 1903. *Roofs of Barcelona* dates from the same year; I like it particularly well because in it I immortalized the view that unfolded before my eyes in the workshop at Riera de Sant Joan.

In one of my several comings and goings to Paris in those years, I had the honor to meet and form a deep friendship with the poet Max Jacob, with whom I shared a room for several months. His happiness and animated conversation accompanied me during many evenings, and his death during World War II left a big empty spot in my heart.

The Rose Period

However, as the saying goes, all things must pass. In the fall of 1904, after I had been settled in Paris for a few months, in a study located in a house known by the name of Bateau-Lavoir, in Montmartre, I met Fernande Olivier, the woman who would become my companion for the next eight years. And that's not all, for she would also pose for me on many occasions. Her presence would give me the necessary strength and courage to move on and learn to love life again.

At that time, Montmartre, the famous section of Paris, was considered the center of the artistic life. The environment in which I moved during those first years in Paris allowed me to know many interesting people, such as the famous poet Guillaume Apollinaire and the Stein brothers. The parties that they organized in their house on Saturday evenings brought together the best artists and writers in Paris. Those sessions were an inexhaustible source of contacts and friendships that lasted for a long time—such as the long relationship that I maintained with the painter Henri Matisse. Do you know who he was?

He was one of the greatest representatives of fauvism—a style that revolutionized the concept of color in art—and like me, he was influenced by African sculpture.

But let's get back to my work. I have already told you that for me, painting has always been a means of expression; that is, in my paintings I tried to create not only an image or a scene, but to communicate my feelings, my way of thinking, and my state of mind. As a result, at the end of 1904 I replaced the blue shades with ochers and pinks, which were more in harmony with my happiness and renewed optimism. I thus opened a new stage in my artistic production: the Rose Period. But the changes weren't limited to color; the figures and the subjects also changed. The outlines of my people became softer, and the paintings were filled with circus artists: acrobats, tumblers... I was very attracted to the circus world, and I had the opportunity to get to know it well, thanks to the hospitality of the members of the Medrano Circus, which was located in the heart of Montmartre. The artist is a receptacle for emotions that come from all over the place: from the sky, the earth, a scrap of paper, a passing shape.

I also experiencesd a new sense of security and peace—at last I was earning money from the sale of my paintings!

Les Demoiselles d'Avignon

In the following years I made some other discoveries that had a profound influence on my work. I don't know if you have ever had a chance to look the masks that African people used in their rites and ceremonies. Do you like them? The first time that I saw them I was very impressed by their expressive force, which influenced the direction of my work for several years. As an example, I must refer once again to the portrait I painted of Gertrude Stein, or to the oil painting that's entitled *Two Female Nudes*, for both of them clearly reflect my fascination with African art.

However, the great turn in my artistic production was yet to come. I don't want to commit the sin of false modesty, so I must say that in 1907, with my work *Les Demoiselles d'Avignon*, I revolutionized the concept of art that had been in force up to that time. But very few people saw it that way. Most artists and art critics in my circle of friends disapproved of it and advised me to abandon the trend that I had begun with so much enthusiasm. Among the few people who reacted positively, one person, the dealer Daniel-Henry Kahnweiler, believed in me and supported me in my new adventure. Thanks to his help, my fame crossed beyond the borders of France and my income increased considerably, so in 1909 Fernande and I moved to a spacious apartment on the Boulevard de Clichy.

But why did *Les Demoiselles d'Avignon* cause such a scandal?
It's very simple: because in that painting I was breaking the
figurative language. I dared to fragment the human figures to
create nearly geometric shapes, in anticipation of what would
shortly lead to Cubism and abstraction. I am always doing that
which I cannot do, in order that I may learn how to do it!

Of course, for many years it was thought that Avignon referred
to the city of that name in the south of France. However, it
really refers to a street in Barcelona with the same name, in
the area where I had lived, and which had a bad reputation
at the time I painted the picture.

Fortunately for me and for the fans of contemporary art, it didn't take long before I could share the Cubist experience with other artists, such as Georges Braque, Juan Gris, and Fernand Léger. One thing we did was to formulate a new language that is defined today as a departure from the linear perspective practiced by Renaissance artists. Instead, we presented objects from different points of view until we changed the image into increasingly tiny geometric shapes.

That painting was followed by others, in which I also began a process of abstraction, and in which any kind of reality sometimes disappeared. And not just paintings; I also put lots of effort into sculpture, experimenting with materials and mixing them into a single work, as in *Mandolin and Clarinet*.

Further Infractions in the Shadow of World War I

My relationship with Fernande was coming to an end. My meeting in the fall of 1911 with Marcelle Humbert, whom I would call Eva, hastened the breakup, and in 1912 Fernande and I separated once and for all.

Eva and I moved that same year to the Parisian quarter of Montparnasse. My passion for her shines through in inscriptions such as "ma jolie" and "jolie Eva," which I put into certain pictures that I painted in that brief but intense period of happiness.

However, as at other times, happiness vanished overnight. In the middle of 1913 my father died, and in August of 1914 World War I broke out. Many of my friends were drafted to fight in an absurd war—all wars are absurd—that would last until 1918 and would claim many innocent victims. But the event that really laid me low was the death, at the end of 1915, of my beloved Eva. With scarcely any time to enjoy our new love, tuberculosis took her life, and darkness and solitude once again took control of my soul.

As an artist, I was fully immersed in the new art movements that flourished left and right, and yet I didn't abandon Cubism. I again made my contribution and started introducing other

elements into my paintings; in other words, I discovered collage. You may wonder, what is collage? It involves adding paper, cloth, cardboard, or other material from our daily surroundings to a composition—including such things as musical scores, wallpaper, and labels from bottles.

Still Life with a Straw Chair was my first contribution to this technique; but my constant restlessness caused me to introduce collage to sculpture, too, so in 1912 I did a three-dimensional composition entitled *Guitarra*.

Paulo

In 1917, thanks to my great friend, the poet Jean Cocteau, I began to collaborate on set and costume design in the dance spectacles of Sergei Diaghilev's Russian Ballet. The staging of *Parade* took me to Rome. There, in addition to having the pleasure of contemplating the remains of ancient classical art and the masterpieces of Renaissance artists such as Michelangelo and Raphael, I met the woman who would become my first wife: the ballerina Olga Kokhlova.

I imagine that my first direct contact with classicism influenced my decision to momentarily abandon the Cubist style and return to figurative art. Did I mention that figurative art usually has human or animal figures as topics? The results of that were paintings such as *Two Women Running on the Beach*. I also rekindled my interest in the harlequin, a character in the *commedia dell'arte*. In those years I painted many of those figures in bright, cheerful colors.

But don't think I took a step backward in my evolution as an artist. Quite the contrary, what I tried was to combine the two languages. As on other occasions, I followed my intuition and my artistic freedom, and in the scenery of the ballet *Parade* and the painting *Three Musicians* I showed how far one can go in combining two very different conceptions of art.

Many things happened in 1918: the World War I finally ended, and I married Olga Kokhlova. The year 1921 gave me the best possible gift: my first son, Paulo, was born. I have done many portraits of him, but if I had to stick with just one portrait, I surely would choose *Paulo Dressed as a Harlequin*.

At that time, the price of my works was on the increase, and that tendency would continue. I became a rich man—a millionaire. I suppose that around that time gossipy tongues began spreading my reputation as a miser; but I must say in my defense that I experienced poverty firsthand for many years, so I tended to place considerable value on financial security.

MINOTAURE

Other Realities

Do you know what Surrealism is? It was an artistic and literary movement that took its inspiration from dreams and the subconscious; it refused to depict the reality that we perceive through our senses when we are awake. In the 1920s I became immersed in the Surrealist environment of Paris, and I met André Breton, the founder of the Surrealist movement and editor in chief of the magazine *Minotaur*, for which I did a cover in 1933. Also in 1920 Joan Miró visited my workshop, and the two of us developed a profound friendship.

My interest in the Surrealist theories and the work of some of its followers, such as the suggestive paintings by Miró and Salvador Dalí, motivated me to do some paintings influenced by this movement, such as *The Dance* and *Seated Bather*.

However, another point of interest was commanding my attention: the figure of the minotaur. Even though I was interested in this subject before my collaboration with the publication *Minotaur*, my obsession was now much more intense. This fascination resulted in a series of engravings entitled *Minotauromaquia* of 1935, in which appear many of the symbols that I used throughout my life, such as the horse and the bull.

But far from feeling satisfied with all these changes and attempts, I also devoted part of my time to sculpture, in which the sculptor Julio González played an important role, and to painting portraits. In the second half of the 1930s I painted many portraits of Marie-Thérèse Walter, whom I met in 1927 and who was my companion starting in 1931, when I separated from Olga. In 1935 Marie-Thérèse gave birth to our daughter, Maya.

In 1935 my childhood friend Jaume Sabartès also came to Paris, and he worked as my secretary for the rest of his days. I don't want to miss the opportunity to thank him with all my heart for his efforts to establish the Picasso Museum in Barcelona, the first museum dedicated exclusively to my work, which opened its doors to the public in 1963.

The Horrors of War

One fateful day in July of 1936, civil war broke out on Spanish soil. I used my fame to publicly proclaim my support for the republican cause, because at that time, until the coup staged by General Franco, Spain had been a democratic republic. Four months later I was named director of the Prado Museum by that government, which was then at war with the Fascists.

But on April 26, 1937, when I learned of the aerial bombardment delivered by the German forces that leveled the Basque town of Guernica, I finally understood the extent of the horror and destruction, and the anguish from sudden, unexpected death.

I immediately set to work, and in a few weeks I completed one of my most dramatic and heartfelt creations: the painting entitled *Guernica*, in honor of the victims of the first indiscriminate air attack in history on a civilian population.

The public had the opportunity to view it at the Universal Exposition of 1937 in Paris, and currently it is displayed in the Reina Sofia Art Center in Madrid. The use of only whites, grays, and blacks creates an atmosphere of desolation. The people and the animals, deformed and fragmented, have their mouths open because they are screaming in horror. The only sign of hope comes from a flower sprouting on the blade of a broken sword.

On January 13, 1939, a few months before the end of the civil war and the start of another much more terrible war, my mother, María Picasso, died.

I can't tell you much more about those years. My relationship with Marie-Thérèse had come apart. Another woman, Dora Maar, shared tears with me for my native country and the even harder experience of World War II, which lasted until 1945. My dear friend Max Jacob was added to the endless list of victims of that terrible conflict: in 1944 he died a prisoner in a concentration camp.

The story is told of how the Nazis visited my workshop during the German occupation of Paris, and when they saw a reproduction of *Guernica*, they asked me, "Did you do this?" To which I answered, "No, you did."

Stone and Clay

The years after World War II were marked by change. My relationship with Dora Maar had come apart, and now I was sharing my life with Françoise Gilot, the mother of my two children Claude and Paloma.

The end of the wars, which had caused so much pain, and my new family situation restored my joy of living, and once again feelings of hope and solidarity blossomed in me. As always, my work and my life are testimony to that transformation: in August of 1948 I participated in a peace convention in Poland, and in January of 1949 I created a lithograph, *The Dove*, which was chosen for the poster for another peace convention that was to take place in Paris in April of the same year.

But what's a lithograph? Do you know? For any readers who may not know, a lithograph is a reproduction, or print, of a drawing that was done in pencil and special ink on a stone or a zinc plate. Thanks to this technique, which I learned in the shop of the French printer Fernand Mourlot, I could create works of art that were not just available to only a few of the wealthy and prominent—the price of a lithographic reproduction was much lower than that of an original. My relationship with lithography was long and fruitful; the proof is the great number of works in black and white and color that I did using this technique, and which today you can see reproduced in many books.

However, the work that best expresses my renewed happiness, my hope, and my confidence in the future is *The Joy of Life*, which I painted in 1946. In it, the subject, the shapes, and the color combine to create a happy, peaceful image of my stay near the sea, in Antibes, where I spent long months of happiness with Françoise.

But once again my active, curious mind compelled me to experiment with new materials and techniques. The opportunity presented itself in Vallauris, in the French region of Provence. There I came into contact with the Ramiés, who invited me to their ceramics workshop and shared with me the secrets of their art. In my hands the clay seemed to take on a life beyond the traditional models that we had been accustomed to. Bulls, plates with almost childish faces, female figures with large proportions, and vases in astonishing shapes burst forth...

And what about sculpture? I used it to show that any material is suitable, and a single sculpture can be comprised of different elements. That is proven by *The She-Goat*, which is made up of discarded materials joined together with plaster.

The Past Comes Back to Life in the Future

I suppose that by now you have deduced that women played a very important role in my life and work. Despite my respect and admiration for them, my sometimes difficult, egotistical, and irritable personality kept me from maintaining a long and stable emotional relationship. I suppose I realized this, but even though I wasn't capable of fully expressing my love and devotion to the women I loved, I was capable of expressing them with my paintbrush. These women who had been at my side left their

faces in my work; they inspired me, and I immortalized them in a thousand different ways.

In 1954 I began, once again, a new relationship with a woman, Jacqueline Roque, who accompanied me in my flight from the mob of journalists and curiosity-seekers and moved with me to our new home in Cannes. In 1961, six years after the death of my first wife, Olga, we got married and we went to live in Mougins, 6 miles from Cannes. Before that, in Vallauris, I did a portrait of her, *Jacqueline with Her Hands Folded*, which is now in the Picasso Museum in Paris. In this painting I wanted to preserve her beautiful profile in a style that, without abandoning figurative art, uses Cubist shapes to highlight and simplify her facial features.

At that time I was very interested in great paintings. Ever since my first visit to the Prado in Madrid, I had been fascinated by the masters of the past and their contributions to the evolution of art.

But that fascination wasn't limited to the artists of the Renaissance and the Baroque, for it also included the ones who came before me in time and style, such as the French painters Gustave Courbet and Edouard Manet. The result of my years of study are the reinterpretations I did of some of their most famous works, such as *Las Meninas* by the Spanish baroque painter Velázquez and *Déjeuner sur l'herbe* by the Impressionist Manet.

But little by little, almost without my knowing it, old age was creeping into my body, if not into my mind and my spirit. I knew that time was drawing to a close, and that there was no going back; so I decided to increase my frantic pace even more.

My last years were characterized by a dizzying production. I experimented with all techniques and all styles. Age and experience gave wings to my hands, which broke all ties that could sap the freedom of my creativity. An example of this work is *Man, Woman, and Child,* which is now in the museum that my childhood city, Málaga, has dedicated to me.

On April 8, 1973, after a long life dedicated to art, my heart stopped beating in my home at Notre-Dame-de-Vie, in Mougins. Two days later I was buried in the gardens of Vauvenargues castle. That's how an intense adventure, begun ninety-one years before, came to an end.

Acknowledgment of a Life Dedicated to Art

Even though I have never placed much value on honors, I must say that, starting in the 1970s, there were many events in which my work was featured.

In 1966 my friend André Malraux, who at that time was cultural minister of the French government, organized in Paris a retrospective exhibit of my artistic production. Five years later, in 1971, the Louvre sponsored another exhibit of my work.

And that's not all. In 1963, as I have already mentioned, the public was first able to visit the Picasso Museum in Barcelona, where paintings that I gave to the museum, drawings from my childhood, and portraits of my friends are displayed.

I also found out that *Guernica* finally reposes in Madrid. Even though it was displayed for many years in the Museum of Modern Art in New York, I wanted it to reside permanently in Spain. My wish was granted in 1981, and now this symbol of the horrors of war is displayed in the Spanish capital.

That's not the end of the honors. In 1985 the Picasso Museum in Paris opened with a large collection of paintings donated by my heirs and enriched by later acquisitions. If you travel to the capital of France one day and visit the museum, you will see beloved paintings that are representative of my work, such as *Family of Saltimbanqus* and *Les Demoiselles d'Avignon*.

But undoubtedly the greatest honor of all came from the city of my birth, Málaga, which in October of 2003 opened a museum with a representative sampling of my artistic production.

Thanks to all for these moments of glory and for displaying my work in the most prestigious museums of the world, such as the Metropolitan Museum of Art in New York and the Tate Gallery in London.

Especially, for allowing me the honor of adding my name and my work to the list of the great masters of art. I want to add only that my art is the result of an evolution begun many centuries before, and of the experimentation and the creative freedom that we artists fostered and carried to their ultimate expression during the first decades of the twentieth century. That period, one of the most prolific of all times, has now passed into history, along with the avant-garde movements and the birth of contemporary art.

Years	Picasso's Life
1881–1900	**1881** Born October 25 in Málaga, Spain
	1891 His family moves to La Coruña.
	1896 *The First Communion*, in the Third Exposition of Fine Arts and Art Industries (Barcelona, Spain)
	1897 *Science and Charity*, in the General Exhibition of Fine Arts in Madrid. Studies at the San Fernando School of Fine Arts in Madrid.
	1898 Returns to Barcelona. Residence in Horta de Ebro.
	1900 Exhibition in the tavern Els Quatre Gats in Barcelona. First trip to Paris.
1901–1920	**1901** Death of his friend Casagemas. Begins his Blue Period. Second trip to Paris. Exhibition in the Vollard Gallery.
	1902 Third trip to Paris
	1904 Moves to Paris
	1905 Begins his Rose Period. Meets the Stein brothers.
	1906 Meets Henri Matisse. Residence in Gósol (Lleida). Portrait of Gertrude Stein.
	1907 Paints *Les Demoiselles d'Avignon*. Birth of Cubism. Meets Kahnweiler, his second agent, and Georges Braque.
	1909 Second residence in Horta de Ebro.
	1911 Summers in Ceret (southern France), a favorite place for Cubist painters.
	1913 Death of Picasso's father.
	1917 Trip to Italy. Meets the ballerina Olga Kokhlova, whom he marries in 1918.
1921–1940	**1921** Birth of son Paulo
	1935 Breakup with Olga. Birth of his daughter Maya from his relationship with Marie-Thérèse Walter. Sabartès becomes his private secretary.
	1936 Is named director of the Prado Museum in Madrid.
	1937 Paints *Guernica*
	1939 Death of Picasso's mother
1941–1960	**1944** Affiliation with the French Communist Party
	1947 Birth of son Claude, from his relationship with Françoise Gilot
	1949 Birth of daughter Paloma, also with Françoise Gilot
	1954 Moves to Cannes with his new companion, Jacqueline Roque
	1955 Death of Olga Kokhlova
	1957 Paints *Las Meninas*
1961–1973	**1961** Marries Jacqueline Roque
	1963 The Picasso Museum in Barcelona opens.
	1966 Retrospective of his work in Paris
	1968 Death of Jaume Sabartès
	1971 Exhibit of Picasso's works in the Louvre, Paris
	1973 Dies on April 8 in Mougins, France

History

1881–1890 Triple Alliance involving Germany, Austria-Hungary, and Italy. Death of Alphonse XII. Second International in Paris. **1891–1900** Wars in Melilla and in Cuba. Assassination of Cánovas del Castillo. Creation of the Hague International Tribunal

1901–1910 First Nobel Prizes are awarded. Alphonse XIII King of Spain. The Sixth Zionist Congress claims a Hebrew state in Palestine. **1911–1920** World War I (1914–1918). League of Nations founded. Russian Revolution breaks out.

1921–1930 Mussolini enters Rome. First National Socialist convention in Munich. Lenin president of the USSR. Crash of the New York Stock Stock Exchange. Peaceful protests by Gandhi. **1931–1940** Hitler Reichs-chancellor. F. D. Roosevelt president of the U.S. Spanish Civil War (1936–1939). World War II (1939–1945).

1941–1950 Japan bombs Pearl Harbor. Atomic bombs dropped on Hiroshima and Nagasaki. **1951–1960** Eisenhower president of the U.S. Warsaw Pact. Elizabeth II Queen of England

1961–1973 Construction of the Berlin Wall. Cuban Missile Crisis. Invasion of Czechoslovakia.

Science/Technology

1881–1890 Edison invents the incandescent electric lightbulb. Height of the telegraph and electromagnetism. **1891–1900** Becquerel discovers radioactivity, Röntgen discovers X-rays. Freud publishes *The Interpretation of Dreams.*

1901–1910 First Mercedes cars appear in Germany. First flights of the Wright brothers. Death of Robert Koch, discoverer of the tuberculosis bacillus. **1911–1920** First uses of neon light. The Ford Model T becomes the first mass-produced car. Amundsen conquers the South Pole. Fleming discovers penicillin, the first antibiotic.

1921–1930 Einstein awarded Nobel Prize in Physics. Charles Lindbergh crosses the Atlantic nonstop. Television is invented. **1931–1940** Flight around the world. The Golden Gate suspension bridge is opened in San Francisco. Death of Santiago Ramón y Cajal and Sigmund Freud.

1941–1950 Fermi constructs atomic battery. The first aerosols appear. First nuclear fusion bomb. **1951–1960** Massive vaccination against polio. James Watson and Francis Crick determine the structure of DNA.

1961–1973 Murray Gell-Mann wins the Nobel Physics Prize. Yuri Gagarin makes the first manned space flight.

Art/Culture

1881–1890 Birth of Charlie Chaplin; death of Dostoyevski. **1891–1900** Rudyard Kipling publishes *The Jungle Book.* Death of Friedrich Nietzsche and Oscar Wilde.

1901–1910 Architectural and decorative style of modernism flourishes. Birth of Jean-Paul Sartre and Simone de Beauvoir. Death of Giuseppe Verdi, Jules Verne, and Leo Tolstoy. **1911–1920** Birth of Miguel Delibes and Heinrich Böll. Death of Rubén Darío, Edgar Degas, and Gustav Mahler.

1921–1930 Birth of Gabriel García Márquez. Debut of *The Jazz Singer,* first sound motion picture. Hergé publishes *Tintin in the Land of the Soviets.* International Expositions in Barcelona and Seville. **1931–1940** Jacinto Benavente, Nobel Prize in Literature. Death of Enrico Caruso, Franz Kafka, and Antoni Gaudí.

1941–1950 Jean-Paul Sartre publishes *Being and Nothingness.* Walt Disney debuts *Bambi.* **1951–1960** Debut of *Welcome, Mister Marshall* by Luis García Berlanga

1960–1973 Death of Georges Braque, Jean Cocteau, and André Breton

My name is...

is a collection of biographies of people with universal appeal, written for young readers. In each book, a figure from history, science, art, culture, literature, or philosophy writes in an appealing way about his or her life and work, and about the world in which he or she lived. Abundant illustrations, inspired by the historical time period help us become immersed in the time and the environment.

Málaga

Picasso

Picasso was born in Málaga (Spain) in 1881. His father, an art teacher, guided the first steps of the person who would become one of the most influential figures of twentieth-century art. Picasso's work, one of the most original of all time (drawings, paintings, engravings, ceramics, sculpture, scenery for ballets, and more) passed through various phases (the Blue, Rose, and pre-Cubist periods, Cubism...). Today it is found in the most important museums of the world, especially in the Picasso museums in Paris, Barcelona, and Málaga, in addition to the Queen Sophia in Madrid, where *Guernica*, a huge canvas that denounces the horrors of war, is displayed.